...for the wind and all whom It enlivens...

Jesus Plays

BRIAN J. SHIRCLIFF

VITALITY

buzz, bliss + books

Jesus Plays: NAKED LITTLE FICTIONS, vol 3
Copyright © 2025 by Brian J. Shircliff
Published by VITALITY buzz, bliss + books LLC
vitalitybuzz.org

VITALITY buzz, bliss + books LLC publishes original creations to grow the mission of VITALITY Cincinnati Inc, a 501(c)3 education-based nonprofit: sharing holistic self-care from neighborhood to neighborhood, person to person, and breath by breath since 2010.

The opinions and ideas expressed herein are those of the author and do not necessarily represent the opinions of the VATRONS of VITALITY buzz, bliss + books LLC or the Board of Trustees of VITALITY Cincinnati. Any errors, of course, are solely the author's.

Every effort has been made to give credit to other people's original ideas through the text itself. If you feel something should be credited to someone and is not, please get in touch through our website and every effort will be made to correct this text for future printings. Thank you!

We invite you to honor your mind, your body, your whole self. Do only what you know to be right for you. While the invitations offered here in this book, on our websites and social media, and in our classes are geared to be gentle and easily modified by the participant to fit the participants' needs, please consult your medical doctor or health professional before undertaking any practices.

ISBN: 978-1-954688-41-4

dedication

Teaching freshman Scriptures for seventeen years gave me the gift and opportunity seventeen times to read much or even most of the Bible over the course of two semesters with this age-group who loves a great story.

Sometime in the late third quarter, having just read many of the prophets' poems/raps composed before and during and after the Babylonian Exile, I introduced Jesus through his sayings and parables— long before reading the gospel stories. This strategy offers a completely different view of Jesus...through what he said (sayings/parables attributed to Jesus), not just what was written about him (stories often wrapped around sayings/parables).

The prophets' raps and poems and Jesus's sayings/ parables sit well together and make a lot more sense stylistically when they are next to each other—after all, Jesus and most of the prophets were trying to deal carefully and cleverly with hierarchically-minded invaders controlling life in their region. These prophets and Jesus cultivated ecstasy in their lives even living within "Empire" by many different names...Assyria, Egypt, Babylon, Persia, Alexander the Great's Greece, Rome.

The Hebrew word NaBYAH that gets translated

as 'prophet' by most English-speaking translators actually means <u>ecstatic</u>, someone who cultivates ecstasy and likely shares it. As with his ecstatic-ancestors before him, Jesus was fond of getting high on the wind/YAHWEH...even when surrounded and controlled by the human-forces of Empire. Jesus's sayings/parables are little doses of ecstatic-experience for all who know. **Jesus Plays** invites us all to know.

In the canonical gospels alone, Jesus has a lot to say, of course. With my freshmen students, I honed in on about 15-20 sayings/parables. One could argue that I had simply picked my favorite sayings/ parables of Jesus. However, as I think you'll discover in **Jesus Plays**, these particular sayings/parables attributed to Jesus share a common rhetoric very different from many of the other sayings/parables attributed to Jesus. And note well, short sayings/ parables are very different from long speeches—in style and function and remembrance—especially when we recall the decades and even generations between Jesus's life/death and the eras when each gospel-writer composed their gospel from oral recollections and/or written sources. Short and clever sayings are easier to remember and can last for generations orally.

Most of the sayings/parables said to be from Jesus are embedded within the Gospels of Matthew and Luke, and a few in the Gospel of Mark. The Gospel of John usually has Jesus speaking in long speeches. Matthew and Luke and Mark have some fascination with Jesus's wisdom to free minds and to wriggle free of oppressors and stand up to human-authorities in the name of God; John most often and most simply is strong on belief in Jesus/God as the key to life with miracle-stories and speeches attributed to Jesus guiding the way to faith.

Pull all the words of Jesus in the canonical gospels (Matthew, Mark, Luke, and John) and extra-canonical sources (Thomas, for instance) and lay them all alongside each other and imaginative patterns begin emerging among a few handfuls of these sayings/parables.

Quickly, it becomes clear that some of "Jesus's" words and even styles of speaking do not fit—and sometimes even contradict—the imagination that seems to gel among some of the sayings/parables. How could that be? Maybe Jesus just changed his mind later in life? Well, many sayings/parables attributed to Jesus reflect more the gospel-writers and their community's unique problems, problems that spurred each gospel-writer to compose their gospel with Jesus as some kind of solution for their problem/community. Gospel-writers of the ancient world would have thought it no big deal to put words into Jesus's mouth in their gospels—as long as those words solve some crisis for their community.

And yet, very curiously, many of the sayings/parables—no matter coming from which gospel—share a distinctive voice, style, and imagination, one that seems surprising and clever and fun and expanding and often funny. Love seems to be at the center of this voice—a love for all.

It might be hard for a person living 2000 years after Jesus to get their mind around the possibility that what was important to Jesus might have differed greatly from what was important to any or even all of the gospel-writers.

Each gospel is a political statement trying to sway people of the gospel-writer's time to the gospel-writer's particular view with the goal of solving a problem.

But Jesus's sayings/parables have a different strategy. Jesus often aims to expand the horizons of his hearers toward a vision of no human being having any extra/special power...with God being the holder and originator of all power...with each hearer of his sayings/parables figuring out what to do next.

In *Jesus Plays*, I've tried to zoom in on these more similar sounding, styling, imagining parables/sayings attributed to Jesus. It's my attempt to let Jesus speak...in a way that I hope modern readers can appreciate and wonder about. I've been wondering about what scholars from the Jesus Seminar in the United States have been saying about these parables/sayings for decades. Those who know will recognize some wisps of their influence in *Jesus Plays*.

Jesus, of course, was not speaking to people living in the 21st century—he was speaking to people living during his time and in his particular area of the world, the eastern Mediterranean seaboard under Ancient Rome's control nearly 2000 years ago.

Those of us who are citizens of democratic and freedom-espousing nations (at least on a local level, at least for many of us)—like the United States where I was born and live—will likely have great difficulty understanding this ancient peasant man Jesus who lived in territory occupied for 800+ years by usually nasty and terror-steeped empires. The Roman Empire, after all, killed Jesus in a brutal, public, torturous way. And Jesus was not alone. Ancient Roman authorities used this same method to kill thousands upon thousands of people (millions upon millions?) to control their ever-expanding reach across the Mediterranean world.

Jesus's sayings and parables will likely give us 21st century people a reason for pause—and a window into the prophetic/ecstatic tradition from which Jesus spoke as his ancestors spoke. After all, ecstasy with the wind—with YAHWEH—is what enlivens each one of us...for all who have eyes and ears and hearts to perceive.

I dedicate *Jesus Plays*...

to all the freshman Scriptures students at St.

Xavier & St. Ursula who read and wondered with me about this wild prophetic/ecstatic strand of the Bible, all who entered the babbling biblical river and let it swirl with their own wild imaginations,

to all the creators who came before us and crafted biblical tales and sayings and parables over at least 9 bible-writing centuries, more and less than 2 millennia ago, and all who have carried forward the heart and imagination of these wild ideas in generative ways for all...

may we all be so bold
to stand tall in possibilities
of real freedom in YAHWEH,

in the breeze that enlivens us,

in the breeze we all share....

actors

Jesus, must have natural brown skin, best if 20-40 years of age

6 other persons who play different roles as needed throughout, with at minimum "person 6" played by a woman

the set

radically simple, just actors, some simple lighting, some costume possibilities

the play

one act, of a varying length of time depending on audience participation

could be performed as written (with nudity) or as a "swimsuit edition" or "underwear edition" (during any parts involving nudity)

after/words

Curtain rises. Play begins with Jesus in line with five others, their backsides to the audience. Jesus is last in line, all of them down by a river, each person awaiting their turn for the local wild man to dunk them in a playfully violent way in the river. How? Although all these people here in this scene are adults, such 'playful violence' might best be understood with how an older child/sibling might dunk a younger child/sibling in a pool and hold them down just long enough for the tiniest bit of panic to arrive, enough to scare the younger child/sibling to swim away and also to want to swim back for another round of sibling-play and another big dunking-gasp.

All on stage are naked but the light on stage makes it not so revealing...just backsides can be seen anyway. The sounds of the breeze over the water are evident.

Each one gasps upon coming up from the water and the lights brighten, an indication of awakening before each one exits. The breeze over the water and these gasps are the only sounds. Perhaps those on stage contribute their wispy noises to create these breezy sounds which get interrupted by each one's gasp breaking through the water, perhaps like the sounds of birth-gasping.

After each person gasps, each 'exits' to the edges of the stage to watch and contribute to the breezy sounds.

When it's finally his turn, Jesus comes up from the water and then remains on stage and stumbles around. Wild man stays and watches Jesus, as if to ensure he's alright, and when he discovers Jesus is alright, wild man silently sweeps his arm around himself across the stage and audience as if to introduce Jesus to all who are here. Wild man then exits with all others except Jesus.

Jesus puts on regular clothes of today, maybe boxers and jeans and a t-shirt, as he notices six people re-entering the stage, all of them now also clothed in simple styles of today.

One sits alone—a man who appears to be sick—and Jesus approaches and sits down and eats with him, as the others on stage are aghast at this, Jesus is oblivious to their ridicules, then Jesus stretches out his hand to the sick man and the man seems to brighten before Jesus smiles at him and walks off to meet someone else.

The pattern repeats. Jesus sits with each of these people: A woman with child. A person with a skin tone different from his. A person of a different nationality/flag as him. A person much poorer than him. A trans/genderbending person. Jesus eats and talks and laughs with each one. The same *experience as with the sick man unfolds with each person...after Jesus parts from each person with whom he sits, each person exits briefly and then re-enters stage and audibly with the others ridicules Jesus for the next person Jesus befriends. "You're sitting/eating with him/her/them?! How dare you! They don't count for anything—how could you?!" And such.*

This all seems too much for Jesus—he grows quite anxious—and he runs away by himself to the desert (others exit) where Jesus takes off his clothes and sits and folds his knees into his chest (fetal, seated) and then feels the breeze on his skin and gets blissed out by it, delights in it visibly...he slowly calms...his body relaxes out of that fetal position as he rolls around and delights and dances/twirls in the breeze, in life...this lasts a good while before...

Jesus *to the audience as he puts on his clothes:* There's life in the wind. And ideas....

(walks from one side of the stage to the other and sits down with others who have gathered there)

Alright, got a good one for you....

You want to know what the place and power of God is like?

(yeses from the group as they lean in for the joke)

It's like a farmer scattering dandelion seeds in their field.

everyone laughs, though differently—some finding it truly funny, others shocked, some laughing at others laughing

person 1, *barely able to contain themself:*
What???!!

person 2:
That's completely ridiculous!

person 3, *laughing:*
Did you say "God's place and power" is like that? No way—

person 4 *very seriously to Jesus:*
I highly doubt you know what you're talking about—

person 1, *still laughing, though discovering something more with it:*
—I mean imagine the conversation between the farmer and their spouse...

acted out comedically by person 5 & person 6 who stand up from the group and nod their heads in agreement with person 1's understanding

person 6:
Well, dear, I think I know what's going to make us rich this year. You know—last year—how we

planted tomatoes and green beans and corn—

person 5:
—yes—yes—it all worked out so well—

person 6:
yup—and this year—<u>this</u> year...DANDELIONS!

person 5:
Whaaaaaat????!??

person 6:
Yes—dandelions—you know all of those fancy restaurants like to serve them in their salads—

person 5:
—but, honey—

person 6:
—and then there's that niche market for dandelion wine—

person 5, *crying:*
—we are going to be so poor—
woe is me—woe is us—

person 6:
—and those dandelion greens—full of all those (*wrinkles up his face*)—nutrients—enough to make your head explode—with their—uh—their—uh their <u>flavor</u> (*as he wilts to the ground in tears, apparently gagging on the imagined/remembered taste*)

person 5, *crying even more, until snapping out of it and standing over spouse:*
You fool—dandelions grow anywhere and everywhere—no one will buy from us when they can get them in their own yard—on the side of the road—<u>any</u> and <u>every</u> road—in the cracks of the sidewalk—every damned place!!!

everyone laughing, including person 5 & person 6

Jesus:
And in my mind, from my experience, such (*sweeping his hands over the whole stage and audience*) is the very place and power of God!

(*Jesus laughs with them as person 5 & person 6 rejoin the group and then when it gets a little quieter...Jesus looking at his hands, remembering*)

I used to tell that one with mustard seeds instead of dandelion seeds. You know, back in the day, in a different land where mustard grew more readily than dandelions. But you probably know that—

person 3:
—"used to"? "Back in the day"? What's that supposed to mean?

person 4:
Hey mister, do we know you? Should we?

Jesus, *stunned that they don't know him as he*

looks at the audience and then pretends for person 3's and person 4's sakes like he doesn't hear any of this and continues on:
Uh—okay—uh—how about this one...?

Wanna know what the kingdom of God is like—what the very place and power and way of God is like?

all persons, *in cat-call unison:*
Sure!
Yup!
Uh-huh!

(a person from the group stands up, acts out everything Jesus says as best they can with the info provided)

The very place and power and way of God is like a woman mixing three measures of flour and adding yeast. *(Jesus makes a drumroll-to-cymbal sound as if this is a joke...but no one laughs, and the person playing 'woman' seems confused by it)*

Oh, that's right. *(speaking for their benefit)* We're all living in ___ *(insert current year).*

So...you wanna know what the very place and power of God is like? It's like this: a woman mixing <u>45 pounds of flour</u> into a big ball of dough—and adding yeast— *(Jesus makes a drumroll-to-cymbal sound again, as this same person goes off-stage to get an imaginary massive bag of flour and dumps it into an imaginary vat where this person adds water and then yeast and then dumps out that massive ball and begins trying to knead it, which eventually requires their whole self wrestling it to the ground, soon with their very sticky self...to which Jesus makes that drumroll sound again and again and again...all on stage laugh...as Jesus recovers from watching the scene...)*

Imagine when the yeast kicks in! *(he drumrolls again as he expands his arms to dramatize the growing of the ball of dough)*

Now this whole thing gets a lot more curious if you know something else. In the ancient Mediterranean world I came from, 2000 years ago, breadbaking was something a father would do with his children.

person 2:
Ancient Mediterranean?!

person 1:
2000 years ago?!

Jesus:
That's right. So how in the world could the very place and power and way of God be like...back then...

a woman
baking bread
by herself

with 45 pounds of bread-dough
and adding yeast?

(*he drumrolls again...and laughs...and points to the
others on stage and the audience as he says...*)

Well? What do you think?

*Jesus facilitates a conversation among all and
"yes—ands" every idea...if no one from the
audience responds, actors from the stage chime
in, eventually Jesus makes these points if audience
does not:*

> Well, if God is limitless—infinite—then God
would indeed include even a woman, by herself,
baking bread, 45 pounds of it, and adding yeast.
Get my drift? (*drumrolls more thoughtfully*)

> An infinite God would have to include <u>all</u>
<u>possibilities</u>—even ridiculous ones like the scene
with this woman and the scene with the dandelion
or mustard farmer.

> Maybe God is delightful too—and funny. It's
possible, right?

*at some natural point in the conversation, when
Jesus and everyone else is laughing, the breeze
blows through*

Jesus *to actors and audience:*
You feel that, right?

the parables and laughter and breeze induce a long, deep trance for actors and Jesus as they too breathe with the breeze and soon begin mimicking the sounds of the breeze...dancing around freely... twirling...rolling like toddlers...all getting blissed out by the simplest of things...minutes go by with this bliss...individually and communally...until they all find a contented stillness—almost meditative— and one person begins whimpering with joy and everyone begins laughing...which only adds to the bliss for a time...

and after it all calms...

Jesus:
The wind is powerful—huh?—full of life!

person 3:
Hey mister, who did you say you are?

Jesus:
You still don't know? (*pauses, searches their eyes for understanding, then when no one offers an answer, says a little sadly...*) I suppose each of us is whoever we need each other to be...

person 3:
Huh?

person 2:
What?

person 1, *using their hands charade-like as if Jesus does not speak English:*
What's your name, man?

Jesus, *befuddled they still do not recognize him and trying to offer hints:*
Used to go by Yeshua—guess it would be more like Joshua in your world—(*still none of the persons gets it*)—but later on people started calling me Jes—

person 3:
—well, I like your style, Yeshua—

person 4:
—well I have some ideas on how to improve your style—though you do remind me of someone— and I just can't seem to place how I know you—

person 3:
—yeah—for sure—were you on that show, Yeshua—

person 4:
—show? A movie or a streaming series?

Jesus keeps trying to speak but can't get a word in

person 2:
—or Broadway maybe—that's why we just kind of recognize you—

person 3 *to Jesus:*
—you seem like the kind of guy who might be able to help me—maybe help me believe in God more. I want to be a believer, sir—could you help grow my belief?

person 2:
Yes—yes—you know, like John did. His gospel.

person 3:
God, I love that gospel. "Believe!"

person 1, *mockingly:*
Believe?! Like Santa Claus? Like the Tooth Fairy?

person 3:
Nah, man. Like believing in God—in Christ—the real deal. You see, in the Gospel of John, Christ Jesus is so powerful—and commanding—and—and such a healer!! He's a miracle worker. All ya gotta do is believe!

person 1:
Bet the real reason you love John's Gospel is you fantasize about being the beloved disciple who lays his head in Jesus's lap—

laughter from group and pointing at person 3

person 6, *laughing and pointing at person 3:*
Sexy!!!

even more laughter from group

person 3:
If it got me into heaven, I'd lay my head wherever—

person 4, *very seriously:*
—uh, that kind of thing definitely does <u>not</u> get you into heaven.

Jesus, *opening his palms:*
Hey...it's a big life...God loves all....

person 3 *to Jesus:*
Yeah, that's it. Something about you definitely reminds me of Jesus in John's gospel—something about you—except that John doesn't have Jesus saying any of those silly parables you keep telling us—

person 4:
—and you're too brown to be Jesus—

Jesus:
—uh, I've been this brown my whole life, you know....

person 3:
Well, John is all about growing believers. I mean, really, could you help me grow as a believer? I—uh—I need something stronger to believe in—

something powerful—otherwise I slip into doing such stupid things—

person 4:
—and saying such stupid things—

person 3:
—so—sir—Yeshua—could you help me believe in Christ a little bit more?

Jesus, *wincing at the word "Christ":*
I could help you believe in yourself more—

person 3:
—nah—it's easier to believe in someone else, or something else—so—so, uh, give us a good word—

Jesus:
—uh, I just gave you two wild little stories—stories that got you all blissed out on the wind—man—that wasn't enough?

person 3:
I need more than that—some laws, rules—something that makes me become a stronger believer—

Jesus, *disappointed:*
—umhmm. Yeah.

person 4:
I could use a whole systematic theological approach

into which those laws all fit and make good logical sense. With God as judge, of course. Or me as judge, if you prefer. (*waits for anyone to react and when no one does, he laughs to defuse the tension*)

Jesus, *rolling his eyes:*
I see...

(*awkward silence as they all stare at Jesus and wait*)

Well I've never found laws all that helpful myself—but stories—stories, they offer a whole world of possibilities—

person 4:
—stories are too slippery—

Jesus:
—those little stories I told—they were original with me—but they aren't a whole lot different from the kinds of stories our ancestors were telling around campfires. Centuries before me.

person 3:
Huh?

Jesus:
You know, Eden and Noah, Abraham and Sarah, Isaac and Rebekah, Jacob and Rachel and Leah and all their kids...the stories about all those wanderers getting high on the breeze, you know, like we just did.

person 1:
Far out, man!

person 3:
So you're saying your stories are <u>like</u> those?

person 4 *to Jesus:*
Whoa! Hey there—be careful there—friend—what did you say your name is again?—*(getting out pen and paper to write it down)* those are big-time stories. I mean, to say you're composing stories the likes of Eden and Abraham and Jacob—that's a tall order. God wrote those stories—

Jesus:
—if you only knew, friend—

person 4:
—and we'd be wise to leave the interpretation of those stories to the likes of Augustine and Aquinas—systematic theologians of their super-smart kind—of a tradition of scholarship—

Jesus:
—uh, I think you're the one needing to be careful there—*(person 4 stunned by this begins taking notes, every now and then looking angrily at Jesus)*

person 3:
—I don't get what you guys are talking about—but—but maybe if you explained how your stories could help me, I could grow my belief in Christ—in

God's kingdom—and get my life together—make my dreams come true—

Jesus, *thoughtfully:*
Well...think about my little stories...they purposefully disorient, they invite your imagination to wander all over the place, they invite you to laugh and let in a little more wind—get a bigger view—

person 4, *writing feverishly:*
—so your intention was to confuse us?

Jesus:
Not exactly. My intention has always been to open eyes and ears and hearts to the Infinite, and in order to do that, you have to leave home.

person 3:
Infinite? You mean math?

Jesus, *growing even more flabbergasted with each idea/sentence he adds here, flabbergasted that they have no idea what he's talking about:*
Not exactly. The Infinite, the unbounded God. The One who exists in love and includes us all whether we believe or not. The ecstatic one—YAHWEH— king of the breezes—of all life—who seeps into you and sustains you—enlivens you and me and everybody—talk about love—about lovemaking—

person 3:
—but I thought God only loved us if we prayed

to Him—and—and with that loyalty God would
answer my loyalty to Him by making me wealthy—
you know—Christianity—what my pastor tells me
Christianity is about—

Jesus, *flabbergasted:*
—so you follow m'Jesus—<u>Jesus</u>—and—and—and
you think that Christianity is about getting rich?

person 3, *as person 4 eyes Jesus carefully:*
Of course. God-given riches. All good things flow
from God in Christ.

Jesus, *wincing:*
I see. (*thinks a moment*) When I say "kingdom of
God" or "God's place and power" or "God's way"
some image probably comes to mind right?

person 3:
Definitely. <u>Wealth</u>. God giving His abundant wealth
to those of us who are humble and faithful to Him.
God knocking down obstacles—like my enemies,
or my own disbelief (*sulks at that*)—whatever
stands in my path to God.

Jesus:
If God is Infinite, can there be an obstacle to God?

person 4:
People create obstacles to God—it's called sinning
against Him. You'd better read your Augustine and
Aquinas—or consult <u>any</u> Christian catechism—

person 6:
—Him? God as "Him." But what if God is a woman—

person 4:
—impossible. Read the Bible <u>and</u> any decent catechism <u>and</u> Augustine <u>and</u> Aquinas. God is male. (*gets in person 6's face*) So get over that woman-idea and save yourself from a lot of trouble, not to mention hellfire.

person 6 pushes person 4 who pushes back

person 3, *breaking up persons 4 & 6:*
I really don't care if God is a man or a woman as long as I get what I pray for—my mansion. The rich life. The easy life. I pray for it every day.

person 2:
You mean all I do is pray and I get it?

Jesus:
Be careful what you pray for...you <u>might</u> just get it.

person 4:
—hey, what's that supposed to mean—are you—are you a communist?

Jesus:
No...I'm just suggesting that mansions could multiply your problems—and the wandering life might be more free—more fulfilling.

person 4, *making a few more notes on his paper:*
Uhhuh, I see.

Jesus, *ignoring person 4:*
Abraham and Sarah, Isaac and Rebekah, Jacob and Rachel and Leah—you've read their stories, right? (*all nod their heads yes*) All these mythic ancestors of ours were wanderers—they had no homes. They walked away from the comforts of the empire for life on the wandering open road—

person 5:
—but why? Who in their right mind would do that?

Jesus:
To be free of the empire. To know God—

person 4:
—but empires are good.

Jesus:
If you're a citizen—with protections.

person 4:
Are you a citizen?

Jesus:
Nope. I've never been a citizen of any empire—

person 3:
—what??!—

Jesus:
—and I highly suggest you try it some time—

person 4, *making a note of this on his paper:*
—hey, how did you get in here? into our country??

Jesus:
Do you know that the word 'Hebrew' literally means bordercrosser? rivercrosser? BorderCROSSER—

person 4:
—but I like borders. They keep things neat. Tidy. Clean. Good people in—bad people out.

Jesus:
The Bible is a tug-of-war between the empire-devotés and those who swim away from empires, those who bordercross.

person 4:
But who wouldn't want to live inside an empire? There's safety within empires.

Jesus:
For everyone?

Is there safety for a slave within an empire?

For a low-wage worker trapped in a role?

For a woman who will never measure up to a man no matter what she does? (*person 6 gestures to person 4 and says "yeah!"*) For a child whose parents are stuck in low-wage roles? Or whose skin-color is not white?

Is there safety within an empire for <u>anyone</u> who is not rich?

For anyone queer or not fitting into the top of the pyramid of power?

For anyone without bodyguards or money to pay a bodyguard?

Empires create hierarchies of who is better and more valued and who is not. Those not at the top are at great risk—until they stand up for themselves and demand equal protections.

person 4, *making a note:*
So you're advocating revolution?

Jesus:
I'm advocating that we awaken people to our shared equality as humans. Hierarchies, pyramids—they hide that truth that we are all made of the same stuff, breathe the same air, all of us <u>sharing life together</u> on this amazing planet.

person 3:
So—is there a problem with being at the top of the pyramid—especially if you worked hard and climbed to get there?

Jesus:
If you had to step on people to get up there? If you had to control people to get there or stay there? (*person 3 considers that*)

person 4:
What's the problem with control—with controlling people—as long as it all ends up for the good?

Jesus *stepping a little closer to person 4 for effect:*
Would you want any of us here controlling you, forcing you to do what we want?

person 3:
But even if we did leave behind empires and their controlling ways—life on the road, being a nomad, man, that's gotta be uncomfortable, even miserable.

Jesus:
Guaranteed to be uncomfortable. And disorienting. And adventurous. It will grow your belief—

person 3, *stunned:*
—wait—what? Life on the road could grow my belief?

person 4 *to Jesus:*
You're being ridiculous. Hey, what did you say your name is? (*writing it down*) And from where?

person 6 *to person 4:*
He said his name is <u>Yeshua</u>—

person 1:
—from the country of <u>Mediterranea</u>. Get with the multicultural program!

person 4:
Could you show me where the country of Mediterranea is on this map?

person 6:
You're so ridiculously mean—and old-school.

person 4, *continuing to write:*
And your name, ma'am?

Jesus:
As the old saying goes..."Our forefather Abraham was among the wanderers, the bordercrossers."

In my old language, that saying would sound like:
AHBRaHaM was an AYBRaYiM. Clever, huh?

Back in my day, playing with sound conveyed more nuanced meanings.

person 1, *seeming a little high:*
Today too, man. Song lyrics. Trippy....

Jesus, *impressed with person 2:*
The music in words...yes! yes! Back in my day, only about 5% of the population could read so—

person 4, *snottily as he disregards his fellow actors:*
—sadly, so very much like today....

person 2:
So why do you keep saying that—"back in my day" and "2000 years ago"?! Are you like a vampire or something? Do you, um, have a taste for blood? *(leans toward Jesus and then away from him)*

Jesus, *laughs, says under his breath:*
Coming from a guy who's been trying to drink <u>my</u> blood for millennia...*(person 4 catches a whiff of it, eyes get big and writes this down too)*

person 1, *now definitely high on something:*
Give us more of that hippie shit—you know—peace and love—that crazy wind—

person 5 and person 6 scramble over to person 1 hoping to get a hit of whatever he has

person 3:
One thing's for sure...peace will come by destroying my enemies—*(wrings hands strangulation-like, kind of comedically)* seems ridiculous but I know a lasting peace is possible if I can get them out of the way—*(stands tall, but speaks so only they can hear)* I want to take down every border and every empire and put someone in charge over it all who sees things <u>my</u> <u>way</u>. We'd all *(points to all here)* be rich!

Jesus, *as persons all react to person 3's plan, person 4 noting all the other persons's excitement:*
Oh yeah?

person 3:
Yeah—can you teach us how to take on "THE MAN", uh, man?

person 6, *laughing, speaking to person 3:*
You talking about yourself again? (*laughter from the group*)

Jesus:
Want to take down your enemies—so you never have an enemy again?

person 3:
Absolutely—

Jesus:
—then love your enemies—

laughter again, all thinking Jesus is kidding, and then they realize he's serious

person 3:
Why do you say this bullshit—people are holding you and me down, man—we're not on the top of the pyramid—we've got to rise up and—and—

person 4, *gesturing to person 3 to quiet down, speaking quietly to person 3:*
—hey—hey—let's see if we can get him to say something we can use—
(*turning to Jesus again*)
Yeshua, please do tell, who <u>is</u> my enemy?

Jesus, *looking him deeply in the eye for a moment, calm in the quiet, and then:*
There was this man. About your age. In fact, he looked a lot like you.

He was walking by himself just over there, on the other side of that building when these guys came outta nowhere...

person 5 stands and persons 1 & 2 & 6 surround person 5, all of them acting it out, person 4 watches the action closely, person 3 looking over person 4's shoulder

person 1:
Would you look at that jacket? *(roughly takes it from person 5, each person takes person 5's clothing piece by piece, each one taking turns to hold down person 5 and punch him)*

person 2:
The shirt is sick. And the shoes are mine. Look at that, my size too.

person 6:
I have my eye on those hot pants.

person 5 now nearly naked, they beat him up and leave him there in the middle of the stage, persons 1 & 2 & 6 exit enjoying their new clothes

Jesus, *lifting person 4 to his feet, they both go and examine person 5, person 3 close behind:*
That's a lot of blood, huh? Doesn't look good. Might be going into shock.

(they watch person 5 for awhile, as if helpless in this drama, as Jesus directs person 4 to stand aside)

And along came a Republican.

person 1 enters dressed as a Republican, stumbles upon the body, nearly trips, examines the body without touching

person 1:
Well shit. Not even sure he's still alive. I—I don't want anyone to think I caused this—shit—I—I better get the hell out of here—(*runs, exits, laughter from offstage and catcalls of "Republicans suck", person 4 cannot believe it*)

And next came a Democrat.

person 2 enters dressed as a Democrat, stumbles upon the body, nearly trips, examines the body without touching

person 2:
Well shit. Not even sure he's still alive. I—I don't want anyone to think I caused this—shit—I—I better get the hell out of here—(*runs, exits, laughter from offstage and catcalls of "Democrats*

suck", *person 4 cannot believe it again, this time shaking his head in complete disbelief*)

And look there—in the distance—(*Jesus points offstage and person 4 looks there*)—someone else—coming here—someone you can't stand—who is it there?

person 4, *looking far, unsure:*
Is it an illegal immigrant? A lawbreaker? Someone who doesn't read? Someone who does not love the finer things in life, like 13th century philosophy? Is it my mother-in-law?

Jesus:
And what do you think any or all of these people will do with this poor person bleeding out and in terrible shock and nearly naked right here on the ground?

person 4:
Those wicked sinners will stomp on this poor man—they'll mess with him—they'll probably even try to take his underwear—and—and—and—(*exasperated by the whole thing, now pacing and crying, his arms folded for fear and comfort*)

Jesus, *to the audience:*
You're all in this too. Who can't you stand who's on the way right here? Get a sharp image in your mind...(*pauses*)

(*to all*) And here the person comes...(*Jesus steps in*

and acts as this person)...and this person is shocked to see that person just like you there on the ground... bleeding out...(*Jesus takes off his shirt and ties it around the worst wound, and lifts person 5 up onto his feet and helps him to a hospital and smacks his wallet down onto the counter to the registration-nurse*)...I—I—found this man in the alley back there—and—and—I'm hoping you can take care of him—and no I don't know who he is or if he has insurance—but here—this money is for some clothes or whatever he needs when he recovers—

person 4, *pacing even more at this as he gets tears in his eyes:*
—no—no—no—absolutely not—
no illegal immigrant would ever do that—no way—no fucking way—no lawbreaker—no unintelligent person—and definitely not my mother-in-law!!!! (*sits down and cries, exasperated*)

Jesus, *with some compassion, to person 4:*
What if our enemies could be better humans than us? (*pauses, speaks to actors and audience*) All the more reason to love our enemies...

person 4, *to himself:*
I don't like this Yeshua guy—and I especially don't like foreigners—even worse colored foreigners who try to tell me the way it is. (*person 4 exits, person 5 hands the borrowed shirt/bandage back to Jesus, persons return stolen clothes to person 5 who puts them on, persons 1 & 2 & 3 & 5 & 6 step*

off stage into audience and sit, a pause begins and Jesus sits in it comfortably, quietly, listening for the faintest breeze, only then does he put on his shirt)

Jesus *to audience and actors in audience:*
Well, you're probably wondering—what if that enemy is <u>not</u> a better person than me—someone who is actively trying to hold power over me...? I mean, imagine the situation.

Someone wants to show me—and everybody else watching—that I am worthless.

How would that oppressor hit me? With a punch?

Nah.... The assumption in a fist-fight is that we are equals and going to duke it out to figure out who is marginally better, the best among equals. *(Jesus shadowboxes the air...as oppressor/person 4 appears on stage and glares at Jesus which stops Jesus's shadowboxing with a chill)*

So how would he hit me, this oppressor here? Huh? If he wanted to show me and everybody else that he's far better than me?
(Jesus and oppressor listen for the audience response until...) ...that's right, he'd backhand me—he'd bitchslap me—show everybody I'm his bitch—that he <u>owns</u> me.

(with oppressor's right hand, oppressor backhands Jesus's right cheek, actors in audience 'ooooohs')

Now what could I do? Huh?

I could pick myself up and go punch him, right? And expect he'd likely go crazy on me in front of all these people who just witnessed him owning me. Could work. But he'll find some way to get back at me. Now or later.

So what could I do that might stop him in his tracks for good? (*waits for responses*)

Yeah, I could kill him. But his buddies (*all actors in audience stand up, arms crossed over their chests threateningly*) would likely come and kill me, and my buddies would kill them, and the next set of buddies or their kids would kill their enemies and on and on and on. Hatfield-McCoys all over again. Generational trauma like this all begun because I didn't take the time to think through some better options for dealing with his bitchslapping me.

So what could I do? Huh?

A long time ago, you might recall I advocated turning the other cheek—(*turning his face and pointing to his left cheek, speaking to person 4/ oppressor...*) And now here—hit me here!

oppressor:
Happy to oblige...(*as he wads up his fist and decks Jesus, who falls to the ground and oppressor hits Jesus again*)

Jesus *gets up, holding onto the left side of his face, speaking to the audience:*
Yeah, that doesn't exactly work today, huh?

A lot of people—wrongly—think what I advocated 2000 years ago was to get beat up. Turn the other cheek. Get beat up for God. Be the better person by being the bloodied person. Wrong, wrong, wrong, <u>fools</u> who know nothing of my old world cleverness!

You see, 2000 years ago, we had this thing with right and left hands. Kind of like why you never shake hands today with left hands, unless you're injured or just don't know any better. I mean, if I go up to you (*goes to an audience member*) and offer my left hand to you to shake when my right hand seems to be fine, you'd probably start wondering what was up with me, right?

In the ancient world when I lived, the right hand was used for shaking hands or even forearms (*demonstrating with someone*) to ensure someone was unarmed. Warriors fought with their right hands. Everyone ate only with their right hand.

Why? Because we wiped our butts with our left hands only—in a world without toilet paper. At a meal, one's left hand handled only the cup, the right hand touched the food.

So...let's rewind the story back to the initial

encounter and imagine we are in the ancient world...when the oppressor just backhanded me with <u>his</u> right hand onto <u>my</u> right cheek to show me and all of you that he owned me, I could then (*both act it out*) say to him, as I turned my left cheek to him, "And now here." (*oppressor backs away startled and looks at his hands and then at the audience, befuddled*)

And why would he back away in the ancient world? Because he just tried to embarrass me with the back of his right hand. And I just called him out on it. How? Because now to smack my left cheek, he'd have to use the inside of his right hand—fight me like a little kid fights. (*mimics a little kid's paddy-cake slaps*) Or he could use his left hand...and in the ancient world one cannot win any fight with one's left hand.

So, you see, in the ancient world, I just leveled the playing field here. (*pauses for effect*)

How about another scenario? (*persons: "yeah!"*) This one works for today's customs just as much as the ancient world's customs.

What if this oppressor here wanted to sue me for everything I've got?

Imagine us standing here in the courtroom...(*one of the persons steps forward from audience acting as judge, other persons step onto stage as jury*)

oppressor, *emphatically, dramatically, pointing at Jesus:*
This guy did this and this and this and this to me—so I sue him here before you all for all he's worth, for everything he's got!

Jesus, *calmly:*
Well, you can have it. Here's my watch (*as he removes and hands over each item to oppressor*), my wallet, my shoes, my socks, my shirt, my pants, my underw—

oppressor, *nervously, as jury begins pointing at oppressor and laughing at how foolish he looks holding Jesus's clothes:*
Stop! No! Stop it right there!

Jesus, *calmly as he hands over his underwear, now naked:*
You said you wanted all I got. And now you do—you have it all.

oppressor, *trying to hand Jesus's clothes back to him, though Jesus has his arms hanging calmly at his sides and the clothes just slide off him to the ground:*
That's—that's not what I meant—I—I uh—

Jesus, *stepping forward, speaking to the audience as oppressor embarrassedly exits and all others exit pointing at oppressor and laughing at him:*
—and now he sees that I'm a human being just like he is, made of the same stuff as him, breathing the

same air as him—and there's no need for him to try to hold power over me. Or over anyone, for that matter.

(*pauses*)

But these strategies—they need to be done with some very deep sense of love. Nonviolence like this is a tactic to awaken oppressor and oppressed alike to recognizing the common humanity we share— not of trying to one-up the oppressor. One-upping anyone only causes more trouble down the road....

(*as he puts on his underwear and pants and shirt, oppressor shows up again with two other military-buddies, all wearing military gear and each carrying a large backpack*)

So how about another scenario from my old world? Remember, my hometown was under the extremely brutal Roman Empire's control. Umhmm. Not pleasant one bit for us noncitizens. Those Ancient Romans were torturers—you've heard of crucifixion, right? How people essentially drown in their own spit there nailed or tied up on a tree, after hanging there naked for all to see.

Well those same Ancient Roman soldiers could pick on anyone they wanted to by law and force that person to carry their pack for 1000 steps—about a mile. But not one step past 1000 steps, or else that Ancient Roman soldier would get in trouble.

Didn't matter what the person might be doing...on the way to take their kid somewhere, on the way to work, on the way to a funeral, no matter.

oppressor *to Jesus as oppressor tries to impress his military-buddies:*
Hey you there—noncitizen—carry my pack.

Jesus, *unbothered:*
Sure thing. (*as he puts on oppressor's pack and begins walking with it and counting out each step*) ONE, TWO, THREE, FOUR...

(*to the audience*) Let's fast forward a bit....

(*back to counting for the oppressor*) NINE HUNDRED NINETY EIGHT, NINE HUNDRED NINETY NINE, ONE THOUSAND! (*oppressor delights with his military-buddies at how he could show his power over Jesus, oppressor reaches for the pack but Jesus refuses and soon continues walking with it*) Well, I quite enjoyed that. Let's keep going. ONE THOUSAND ONE, ONE THOUSAND TWO, ONE THOUSAND THREE—

oppressor:
—give me my pack back!

Jesus:
Nah, I'm quite enjoying it. ONE THOUSAND FOUR, ONE THOUSAND FIVE—

oppressor, *freaking out as he tries to grab the pack and save face before his military-buddies who are laughing at him uncomfortably:*
—give it back to me—

Jesus:
—ONE THOUSAND SIX, ONE THOUSAND SEVEN, ONE THOUSAND EIGHT—I'm quite enjoying this— the workout—the fresh air—being with you guys— ONE THOUSAND NINE, ONE THOUSAND TEN—

oppressor:
—give me my pack—now—dammit—(*as he wrestles Jesus to the ground and takes the pack from him while his buddies point at oppressor and laugh at him and others walk over and point at oppressor and laugh too before eventually everyone except Jesus exits*)

Jesus, *still on the ground, catching his breath, eventually talking directly to audience:*
Let me just catch my breath here a bit... (*enjoying the breeze, once he recovers he sits up*)

Nonviolence. It's like jujitsu. Accept the first hit but never allow any other hits.

All you do is hold up a mirror to the oppressor's attempt to hold power over you. And if you do it with some sense of love, things could change.

What do you say? How might it all work today?

(begins a conversation with the audience...if no one says anything, an actor/person could pop up and offer a thought...at some point Jesus must make these points in the conversation:)

> You see, you've got to bring this nonviolent idea into the present. Those ideas we just unpacked here, those would have worked 2000 years ago—because these strategies—especially the first one—played on the assumptions and customs of that time long ago. Today is kind of different, right?

> All the more reason to be inventive, creative, when oppressors try to hold power over us. Just when you think you've got nothing, ask the breeze to give you an idea. And trust that something will come....

> At the very least, remind the oppressor that you are a human being—just like them. That there's no reason to hold power over you or over anyone.

(lastly)
> But nonviolence must be used with love in mind, love for the oppressor. You're trying to show the oppressor that you both are equals under God, that you both and all humans share in this one-same breeze of life...and from this co-equal awakening, you both can move forward in life *(allows a long dose of time to pass before two actors enter and one says:)*

person 3:
Hey man, you work up any more good parables? any more jokes?

person 4, *to person 3:*
I don't like his jokes...

Jesus, *to both of them:*
I should ask <u>you</u> if you've created any parables...

person 3:
Nah, nothing like yours.

Jesus:
Well, time for you to get creating...listen to the wind long enough and all kinds of clever things show up.

person 3:
Come on, man, give us something good.

Jesus:
Oh alright. Have I told you this one? *(two persons enter the stage, one religious looking, the other a street person, each acting as Jesus tells the story)*

Two people went into a house of worship to pray, one was a devoted follower of religion, the other one was a terrible sinner in any and every religion.

The religious person said—out loud—

religious person *speaking to the room and the heavens:*

Thank you, Father God, for making me me. Thank you especially for not making me like other people—like thieves and drug addicts and even this pathetic street person who obviously doesn't know how to pray—I mean, that's why he/she is poor. As you know, Father God, I pray to you so, so often. Every day. That's why you've given me wealth. That's why I sacrifice so much and give 10.17% percent of my income back to pay for this place where they let anyone—it seems—come in here and pray. I even fast on Tuesday between 9:45am and 12 noon from all the delicious food I have in my house that I work for and I pay for to show you, Father God, how much I love you! So, so much! I love you, Father God! I love you!

Jesus:

But the street person just knelt there in the corner—tears in their eyes—not even able to raise those eyes—

street person:

—oh God—please help me—please forgive me—sinner that I am—

person 3 laughs thoughtfully, street person and religious person exit

person 4, *befuddled:*

How is that a joke? Your stories only make me mad.

person 3, *still laughing:*
The way it is. A lot of the time. Sad to say. That was a good one, Yeshua.

person 4, *mockingly, mostly to himself:*
"Yeshua." More like "No-Shua." (*laughs to himself*)

person 3 *trying to explain it to person 4:*
Look, man, you'd think the religious person would be humble before God—in the house of worship—being humble before God is what any and every religion teaches, right? But the humble one here is surprising—

person 4:
—that religious person should have kicked the freeloader out of that chapel—I mean—look—the religious person PAID FOR that chapel—and he/she fasts—

Jesus:
—aw, come on, man, love—what about love—

person 4, *flustered:*
—I don't want your love—not from someone like you anyway....

as street person and religious person re-enter, sheepishly, and begin talking with Jesus, person 4 converses with person 3 at the edge of the stage, then religious person exits in a huff, angry about something Jesus must have said as persons 3 & 4 both stop religious person who points back to Jesus as the three converse

all this as Jesus seems to be offering healing/ consolation to street person before street person exits feeling better

person 3, *pushed forward by person 4 and religious person:*
Yeshua—hey Yeshua—we have a problem—with who you hang around with.

Jesus:
Who—what's the problem?

person 3:
We'd prefer it—we'd like to screen who it is you are hanging out with. No more street people. Instead, more people like us—

person 4:
—smarter people, for sure. More religious people. Cleaner people too.

Jesus, *smiling at the audience, then responding to persons 3 & 4:*
Oh yeah?

person 3:
We'd like to help you, Yeshua—

person 4:
—let's call you "Joshua" though. Easier for people to—to—appreciate you.

person 3:
Yes, with all those good stories you tell (*person 4 rolls eyes*), we'd like to to help you build a movement—

religious person:
—one that lasts.

person 3:
You see, you remind us of someone—

Jesus, *slyly:*
—oh yeah?

person 3:
And he nearly conquered the world—

Jesus:
—well, I'm not about conquering.

religious person:
But you could be taught how to conquer—

person 3:
—it's your message. It's, uh, it's nearly on point.

person 4:
And we'd like to help you shape it to a very fine point.

person 3:
Because—because—there are some things you've been saying that could get you—and us—into serious trouble with the authorities—

person 4:
—and if you took our advice and tweaked your message a little bit (*says these next words behind his hands so no eavesdropper could hear*) we think you might be able to topple those authorities—

Jesus, *loudly as person 4 tries to shush Jesus down:*
—and if we toppled those authorities you have in mind, what would you have me become then? King of kings? Lord of lords? The ruler of all?

person 3, *quietly, nodding:*
Yes. Yes that's exactly it.

religious person, *also quietly:*
And we'd all bow down to you!

person 4, *not quietly at all, much to the shock of person 3 and religious person:*
And we'd be your council of advisors and, you know, tell you what to say and how to say it—we'd protect you, provide you support, garner support among the people. For you.

person 3, *kind of quietly, carefully:*
For us all. We'd rally behind you and encircle you with power.

Jesus:
I thought power comes from God alone.

person 4:
The only thing you'd have to change would be your message—and—and your name—(*as he frowns*) and maybe change your clothes so you don't look so brown. (*turns to person 3*) Maybe we try some makeup on him, lighten his tone?

religious person:
—or maybe we always have him standing in front of a slightly darker background so he appears lighter—you know—when he gives speeches—

Jesus *to both person 4 & religious person:*
—wha—

person 4:
—and this whole business of loving enemies—that doesn't work, Joshua. Enemies—you see—the only logical response to an enemy is to kill them. They must be killed. Destroyed. Obliterated.

person 3:
Blown right out of the water. Out of the air. Toppled from their flimsy thrones. In the name of God.

Jesus:
You think God is about killing?

person 4, *shaking his head at Jesus's stupidity*:
You really think loving one's enemies changes anything? I mean, look at history—

Jesus:
—yes—do look at history.

person 3:
Wha—

Jesus:
—even recent history!

person 3:
What do you mean?

Jesus:
Look at Gandhi! Less than 100 years ago, Gandhi led "experiments with truth" that awakened the oppressing British invaders to realize they could no longer govern India, so the British invaders left.

Look within your own country to Martin Luther King and Bayard Rustin—the Montgomery Bus Boycotts—the Civil Rights Movement—

person 4, *grumpily*:
—please don't remind us—

Jesus:
—King sent Rustin to India to study what Gandhi and the Indian people had done, what worked for

them. And Rustin brought those truth-ideas to the US. And they worked—

religious person:
—but Gandhi wasn't a Christian—how—how—

Jesus, *ignoring religious person's ridiculous comment:*
—plenty of examples of nonviolence working—all over the world—no matter someone's religion—

person 4:
—but King never became a king—and neither did Gandhi—

Jesus, *exasperated:*
—that's exactly the point! That's the whole point! Nonviolence awakens kings and presidents and CEOs and religious leaders to the ultimate realization—that they have no real power that lasts—that royal systems and hierarchical systems of any and every kind are foolish—<u>foolish!</u>—when we are all humans—all of us equals.

person 4:
Joshua, my dear friend, you know deep down that some of us are just better than others. I mean, look around you. That street person—equal to me? Come on, man. Look at him! For Christsake! Those of us who are better must rule. For the good of that street person. For the good of all.

Jesus, *after a long pause staring deeply into person 4's eyes, maybe wondering what could help person 4 realize his own foolishness:*
Look, I appreciate your ideas and concerns—but I'm not the guy to do what it is that you think must be done.

religious person:
It's inevitable, Yeshua—Joshua—<u>Joshua</u>—you'd be smart to lean into it. (*pleading*)

person 3:
You can be THE GUY. Ruler of the whole world, man.

person 4, *coyly:*
We just want to help—

person 4 is interrupted by street person who returns with another street person who is ill and bowed down and reaches out to Jesus, who turns away from person 3 & person 4 & religious person

Jesus sits down with the street people and talks as person 3 & person 4 & religious person exit with some heated unheard words and gesturing angrily back at Jesus

person 1 enters and watches both street people stand looking healthy and happy and grateful to Jesus

Jesus notices person 1 looking amazed with him as street people exit

Jesus:
Why are you looking at me like that?

person 1:
Um, hello—you just <u>healed</u> someone—I—uh—I—was watching....

Jesus:
That—uh—you do know that that had very little to do with me, right? *(persons 2, 3, 4, 5, and 6 enter as themselves hearing the exchange, all of them confused, person 4 is wearing a necklace with a gold cross which he twirls between his fingers in a showy way and making sure Jesus sees it)*

Listen, I think it's time you go off and figure it out for yourselves, each one of you. The reliable ways of God—

person 4:
—not another one of his bright ideas!

Jesus:
How about pairing up—go off and—and—take nothing with you for the journey—no coat, no luggage, no credit cards, no phone—

person 2:
—no phone???!

Jesus:
No phone. Trust that what you need will come to you. When you're hungry or thirsty or need a safe place to sleep, or a shower, or whatever you <u>really</u> need, someone will be generous with you. Rely on their generosity. And offer your gifts too—

person 3:
—but how could we offer gifts—you told us to take nothing with us—

Jesus:
—the best gifts are within you—they come from within you—your presence—

person 1:
—I like presents—at Christmas—really anytime—

Jesus:
—your <u>presence</u>—<u>being with people</u>—it alone is healing—though if someone approaches you for healing, trust that God will flow through you—

person 3:
—but—but—we saw you do it—what makes you think that we can—I mean—you—you're—

person 4, *twirling the gold cross:*
—yes—who are you, Joshua—

Jesus:
—hey, there's nothing all that special about me.

And going on this adventure together you'll find that out real quick.
(*looking them each deeply in their eyes*)
Ask—you'll get what you need.
Seek—you'll find it.
Knock—the door will swing wide open for you.

person 4, *to the others:*
Notice he said nothing about belief—or about God—you really trust this anti-Christian crackpot?

Jesus, *ignoring person 4:*
Listen up here—
catch it from the beginning—
what's the need to believe when
<u>you</u> are the light of the world?

<u>You</u> are the salt of the earth—the spice of life—just as much as I am, as any living and breathing human being is.

Be the light—
shine your light....

So go on. And come back in a few days and tell me about it.

twirling his gold cross between his fingers and making sure Jesus can see it, person 4 circles Jesus before going off with others...Jesus seems repelled by the cross, person 4 seems pleased with himself that Jesus noticed persons split up in pairs or threes, person 4 acts like he's going to join a group but then splits off by himself and spies on Jesus, Jesus goes the other way of the persons, to the solitary desert on the edge of stage and then a lonely cross is illuminated on the horizon...

Jesus, *to the audience, anxiously, unaware that person 4 is on the stage-edge listening:*
You know (*pointing to the illuminated cross behind him*) I was tortured on a cross by madmen, by religious fanatics living within an empire known for its brutal ways of suppressing foreigners and noncitizens. (*pauses and lets that sink in*)

Why people would wear crosses in my honor and think I'd be thrilled about it—just doesn't make sense to me.

I mean, I get the whole idea of celebrating that I lived through my brutal death—

I was—I was killed by torturers—(*extremely anxiously*)

and I was raised up into new life by Love Itself— (*more calmly*) the One who raises us all to life—

but people wearing crosses so proudly and remembering me by the bloody scene of the crime seems more than gross—know what I mean?

Maybe their fascination with my death is one of the reasons they can't hear what I'm saying, dead or alive. (*person 4 is shocked by all of this, takes notes to use against Jesus, like before*)

God knows, if you watch violent show after violent show—delight in violent video games—
play or watch violent sports—even have some sense of belonging by sharing violent things—
of course you'd side with the cross and my brutal death—and forget completely about my life—
about my words—(*putting it all together for himself*)

and that cross—that cross is where they tortured me—where thousands upon thousands were tortured—I—I saw it growing up—all those people—hanging there, soffocating (*points to the cross again, begins vomiting thinking about it all*)—

this violence is an addiction—then and now—only deadlier now. The ones who turned me into their savior to take on empires like Ancient Rome soon became Rome. Kill empire and become it.

(*anxiously, shaking*)
—it doesn't have to be this way—it never had to be this way...(*sits for a long while trying to soothe himself, anxiety turning to confidence as the breeze blows*)
—underneath every addiction is a hunger—a genuine hunger—for life—for love....

Jesus sits, the sun goes down and comes up, via the stage lights, actors all return from their disparate journeys, all loud with each other and more confident in themselves, person 4 rejoins them and acts like he was with them all along...the illuminated cross fades away and the fun spirit of the group improves Jesus's mood even more

Jesus:
Well would you look at all of you, positively glowing.

person 1:
Just when I needed something to eat, someone gave me something—

person 2:
—yeah—and this guy gave me a cup of coffee just minutes after I realized I was thirsty and needed to be warmed up from the rain—I mean, I'd just said to myself, "Gosh, how I'd love a cup of coffee right now."

Jesus:
Love it. God's flowing economy—

person 4 *to Jesus:*
—whoah—whoah—hold it right there, man—Joshua—this—this sounds communist—

Jesus *to person 4:*
—sharing gifts is communism? (*pauses, dumbfounded*) With all that classical training, you do know what the word "economy" means, right?

person 4 gets angry and makes note of this exchange of words on his ever-filling paper

person 5, *excitedly:*
And—and—I put my hands on this guy's injured foot—with his permission—and—and—he said it felt better—

person 4:
—wait—the guy <u>said</u> he felt better or said he <u>was</u> better? Those are different things entirely. And—and did a doctor evaluate this guy's foot and determine if it was truly better or just felt better?

person 1:
What's the difference—he <u>felt</u> better so he <u>was</u> better...?!

Jesus:
God's economy again—the flow of life—

person 4, *genuinely:*
—uh—this all makes me very anxious—Joshua—how—how does all of this work—this whole healing thing—shouldn't someone have a license or certification or something? I mean—

Jesus:
—or you could just trust God—and how God flows through people—

person 4 looks very scared

person 3:
—now I get it—just like you sent us out there to figure it out—I trust in <u>you</u>—I believe in <u>you</u>—

Jesus:
—and I'm a human being—just like you—and <u>you</u> healed—so—

person 4:
—oh you're not quite like us now are you?—you're very different from us—you're brown-skinned with a ridiculous foreign name—
(*turning away from Jesus and toward the other persons*) you know—I feel like 2000-year-old Joshua-Yeshua here is not telling us something—

Jesus:
—you know, as I've told you, I've been brown my whole life—2000 years in fact—and as for my name—

person 3, *getting uncomfortable, taps person 4 to quiet him down, then changes the subject:*
—we were talking—you know—while we were away—we were all talking about who you are—

Jesus:
—okay—alright—so who do you say I am?

person 1, *acting kind of high all the sudden:*
You're like some wild reincarnation, man, of that naked nature-guy who dunked you in the river—

and got you all high—(*Jesus bewildered by that as are the rest of the persons who tease person 1*)

Jesus:
—oh—right—high—high on the wind. (*as others laugh*) The <u>wind</u>!

And uh, you all were there when the wild man dunked me—so he and I couldn't be the same person, right?

person 2:
Well, you are a prophet—like a shaman—with special magical powers. You know, you heal people.

Jesus:
Well that describes all of you now, huh? A bunch of healers. (*lets them consider that*) Any human breathing in the life available to all in the air can heal. YAHWEH—

person 5:
—you're divine—the son of God.

Jesus, *a bit uncomfortably:*
Well <u>I</u> <u>am</u>—divine—just as I told you <u>you</u> are divine, all of us swimming in the Infinite God. <u>You</u> are the salt of the earth—the spice of life—the light of the world—we're all divine—

person 3, *getting feisty with all of this, standing:*
—dammit—stop playing around—you're the

Messiah—the Christ! The one who heals—who makes us whole—the one in whom we are putting our trust—to take down the forces of Empire that kill us slowly—that divide us—that break us down—you—you are the Christ who will establish a new empire of all empires here on earth—I believe in <u>you</u>, man—<u>you are the Christ</u>—

Jesus:
—whoah—tell no one that! No one!

(siren-lights, all persons except Jesus freeze, all lights dim except spotlight on Jesus who speaks directly to the audience)

Whoa—whoah—whoah—hold it right there— that's what I said, back then 2000 years ago and just now too. "Tell no one that!"

Look it up.

Why would I say such a thing? Huh?

I mean, most people who think they're following me call me "Christ." But I told my friends back in the day 2000 years ago not to call me Christ.

(pauses)

Why?

Well, as I reminded you just a few minutes ago, I

was executed by the Roman Empire, with the full participation of the religious authorities of my own religion. All of them were hierarchical-fanatics.

This whole Christ-business has more to do with the values of those who killed me than it does with what I've shared here today/tonight.

Perhaps this surprises you?

Well, what is a Messiah? What is a Christ—that I wouldn't want to be called that?

Messiah is a Hebrew word—means "oily one"—someone who has been smeared with oil. Most references in the Hebrew Bible to "messiah" are in 1 & 2 Samuel—"messiah" being a title reserved for anointed kings like King Saul and King David.

A lot of people think David's a good guy....

But both Saul and David are nasty, self-centered characters. Read it for yourself in 1 & 2 Samuel. They're so nasty that the priests will completely re-write David's and Saul's stories in 1 & 2 Chronicles to make them into more reasonable characters— with a heroic David in their sanitized Chronicles.

But the writers of 1 & 2 Samuel—they want you to see that Messiah Saul and Messiah David are nasty and far from heroes. They kill women and men, they kill children and elderly. They are genocidal maniacs intent on growing their own power and prestige, no matter the cost.

What's the Greek word for "messiah"? It's <u>Christ</u>.

Messiah Saul & Messiah David. Christ Saul & Christ David—I do <u>not</u> want to be associated with them. If you know what's good for you, you won't either.

And only you know what's good for you....

one more spin of the siren-lights then stage-lights come back on, all characters unfreeze

person 3:
You are the Messiah—you are the Christ—

Jesus:
—don't you dare call me that—don't put that nastiness on me—

person 4, *clearly interrupting and trying to talk over Jesus:*
—hey—hey—Joshua—don't ya think a guy as clever as you should be rich? I mean, if you're so powerful and important, you should make God rain down His abundance upon you—
for your own self—

Jesus:
—you mean upon <u>your</u> own self? I want nothing to do with that.

person 4:
—but—but—homelessness—it's just not sexy—

Jesus:
—I <u>choose</u> to wander, I <u>choose</u> to cross borders, like my ancestors wisely did—follow the life in the wind—

person 4:
—but—but our lives could be easier—your life could be easier—more comfortable—we'd protect you—and build that movement to put all rulers under your feet—our feet—you could rule—

Jesus:
—no!—absolutely not—I want no part of that—

person 2:
—yeah—I'm tired of living like this—I want my mansion—I want the easy life—

person 1:
—I want a better car—something nice—

person 2:
—yeah—something fast—

person 3, *trying to rile up the others to join him:*
—Joshua, if you'd only let us look out for you, let us make you into someone powerful—you could—we could have that mansion—each one of us—and all those cars—and—and—

Jesus *to person 3:*
—absolutely not—and that mansion you seek
is <u>now</u>—is <u>here</u>—*(gestures to the Earth around
him)*—just as the heaven you seek is here—is
now—

*person 3 gets frustrated with Jesus and signals to
the others to leave with him, all exit and bond with
each other over their shared concerns, all except
Jesus*

Jesus *to the audience:*
Beware.

Beware of anyone putting one person above you or
below you—or them—or anyone—that game—it's
fascism through and through—

*all other actors return as oppressors, all wearing
white robes with pointy hoods over their heads/
eyes and neck-gaiters up over their noses and big
wooden crosses around their necks—they crowd
in around Jesus, the big cross gets illuminated
downstage again, as oppressors surround Jesus*

Jesus, *working hard to make eye contact with each
one through their hoods:*
Hoods and crosses—
oh please—in ___ *(insert year)*?!

person 4:
—you will be our perfect sacrifice—if you won't kill

for us as ruler over all the Earth then truly we'll kill <u>you</u>—in the name of God—

person 1:
—God will raise you up for us as our Lord of Life—

person 2:
—and Lord of Death—

person 3:
—dying you destroy <u>our</u> death—rising you restore <u>our</u> life—Lord Christ—come in glory!

person 4:
Glory! GLORY! A holy Christian nation!
A people pure and set apart!

person 2, *echoing:*
Dying you destroy our death—

person 5:
rising you restore our life—

all actors except Jesus, *repeating the lines in unison a few times and then in rounds as they sing and and circle around Jesus, every now then crowding in closer:*
—dying you destroy our death—
rising you destroy our life—

Jesus, *finally:*
—STOP! STOP!!! We're not doing this again! To

anyone! I'm a human being—just like you! You are not killing me—

person 4:
—oh yes—yes we are—

Jesus:
—people just like you did that to me 2000 years ago—wake the fuck up! Wake—the—fuck—up!

(*singing, as they try to ensnare Jesus with their white robes and strip him of his clothes and enrobe him as they are robed, Jesus does not cooperate*)

<u>You</u> follow Jesus?! Such a disgusting thirst for killing and cruelty among so many Christians—why?! What happened to you all? What—

person 4:
—ah, you see, it's God's economy—we kill you and God loves us all the more. Check out your history on that one, "Joshua."

Jesus:
You really think that?! You can't be serious—

person 1:
—go set up a room in your heavenly mansion for me—

person 2:
—and me—

person 5:
—and me—

person 4:
—<u>you</u> are our perfect sacrifice—brown skin is perfect for—for what we need here—(*uses the back of his own hand to brush Jesus's face, remembers it's the same hand he used to backhand Jesus earlier and replays that slowly with little backhand smacks on Jesus's face to person 4's own delight, other persons hold Jesus's arms and legs, Jesus breathes heavily and anxiously and tries to calm himself, person 4 is roused from his slapping-reverie by the next rounds of the refrain as he joins in...*)

person 3:
—dying—

person 1:
—you destroy our death—

person 3:
—rising—

person 4:
—you restore our life!

person 6, *trying to leave:*
I don't want this—any of this—

person 5, *pulling person 6 back:*
—stay—you'll be rich—

Jesus:
All of this even after you all experienced life and healing flowing through <u>you</u>! Within <u>you</u>!! God's life and love—<u>in</u> you! Each one of you—

person 4, *as cross brightens in the background:*
—we will all be washed clean of our sins—through the blood of the lamb we slaughter—right here—right now—

all oppressors except person 4, *whispering in the background over and over again:*
—dying you destroy our death—rising you restore our life—

Jesus, *shaking his head and trying to wriggle free of their grasp on him:*
No. Absolutely not.

person 4, *to Jesus as he unhoods himself:*
You know this is right. Don't you?! <u>Jesus</u>...

Jesus, *shocked, to person 4:*
You mean to tell me—you know me as Jesus—THE JESUS—and you still act this way?!

person 4 laughs at him and at the whole situation as the rest continue to hold Jesus by his limbs, some try to ensnare Jesus with their white robes and strip Jesus of his clothes and enrobe him as they are robed

person 4, *stepping outside the whole group/mob and holding up the piece of paper upon which he's been writing through the whole play, background chant "dying you destroyed our death, rising you restore our life" continues quietly as the rest of the oppressors encircle Jesus, person 4 outside the circle says:*
Right here. Right here, Jesus, I've been recording your words, your sayings, your stupid parables.

Right here is enough evidence to have you put to death for treason—you're a traitor against this nation—Jesus—you're a traitor against our <u>Christian</u> nation—

you Jesus are a traitor against the Holy Church who worships you every Sunday (*Jesus rolling his eyes*)—against the Holy Church of Holy Thomas Aquinas—against the Holy Church who prays to you every day—who <u>fasts</u> for you—

how disgusting of you to turn your back on your Church—on this nation—<u>you</u> <u>must</u> <u>die</u>, Jesus!!!

(*mob of oppressors build the speed of their circling and the sound of their chant for a few seconds and then they quiet as person 4 continues...*)

but we could stop your killing—yes—yes—we could stop it—all that torture—if you'd just pledge your allegiance to me—to us—(*as person 4 points to the hooded ring of persons encircling Jesus*)

Jesus, *ignoring person 4, looking person 1 and person 2 in the eye, pulls the hood and gaiter off each one and makes deep eye contact with each one:*
I am Jesus. (*then shouting*) I am Jesus!!!

person 2:
—but what about my mansion?

person 1:
—and my car?

Jesus, *eyes raised, simply:*
I am Jesus.

person 1 and person 2 exit, disappointed, then Jesus turns to person 5 & 6, unhoods them

Jesus:
I am Jesus. (*then louder*) I am Jesus. I have always been Jesus.

person 5 and person 6 exit, disappointed, then Jesus turns to person 3 & 4, unhoods person 3 who seems disappointed by this and disappointed in person 4's plan, person 3 pulls his own gaiter down

person 4:
Well, Jesus, are we going to have to kill you again to make you worth anything to us? Or will you finally let us crown you and encircle you with power—alive—to conquer the world as the living Christ, the universal Christ we all want you to be for our

One Nation Under God...our Holy Christian Nation of <u>Jesus</u> Christ, Victor over the whole planet?

Jesus:
Don't you dare use my name like that—
never for your personal gain—
(*shouting*) what do you think God will do with you?!
Do you hear me—(*even louder*) what do you think God will <u>do</u> <u>with</u> <u>you</u>?!

Stunned by the question, person 3 exits dejected and looks at person 4 for guidance but person 4 offers none, person 4 then slowly exits thinking about what Jesus said. Turning to the audience, Jesus is spotlit on the stage, as the wind blows the illuminated cross fades away.

The wind howls and then settles. Jesus recovers, soothes himself, soothed by the wind, then says...

These are desperate times.

What we need now is a whole generation of Jesuses who <u>stay alive</u>, who stand their ground in Life, in the Truth of Life—no matter the torturers who stand against them. Against us.

Once again, some very misguided men and women will use my name to try to kill, to try to dominate the Earth.

Yes, they've done this in every generation.

But this time it's different—

if—if we're not careful, it will become World War 3 with weapons that could destroy any chance for much human life on the planet.

That sick title of Christ will be used to justify the killers' violent actions and their out-of-control greed.

Surprised by that?

I mean—seriously?!?!

Look at recent history—Nazi Germany and the Ku Klux Klan were <u>Christian</u> movements. That's right. Nazi Germany even had "God With Us" engraved on their belt-buckles.

(pauses to let it sink in)

Of course, today and in their primes, the Nazis and the KKK would have killed me too. And fast. To shut me up before more of my 2000-year-old sayings gain any more traction.

And then they'd make me the Risen Christ again to use me for their own gain—and to shut me up. Make my story—what they did to me—more important than my words, my ideas.

The same misguided thinking that killed me 2000 years ago killed Gandhi. The same misguided thinking that killed me 2000 years ago killed MLK.

You'd better start thinking...or you'll—
you'll be next. (*long pause, long eye contact with the audience*)

We gotta do better—better than I did my first go-round, better than Gandhi and MLK did. Stay alive!

(*pleading with the audience*) You can stop this violent madness. All of you together.

How to even begin? Well....

There's a huge difference between Christ and Jesus, between Christ and me. There's a huge difference between the violence of killers and the world-transforming love I'm espousing.

Learn to discern the differences between killing and loving. Today's religions all have killing and loving intertwined together. Many governments too. Even most families. We keep passing on this confusion and violence to each generation.

To live, to last, we all must disentangle killing from loving.

We must stop saying killing and loving go together. They do not! That's a trap with no winners.

Study my sayings, my lifestyle, my rhetoric and

way of speaking, sure—yes—but even better, learn from the wind, as I did, as I do. Play with the wind. Dance with It. Let It dance you into life.

Stand your ground with love, with life, with all you are. Yes, being a person of love is a risk—but the risk—the risk of doing nothing could be far greater.

Talk to each other. You all'll find ways that work. Together. The wind will feed you ideas. That's what YAHWEH is—the wind. Ask the wind to help you.

(*soothingly*) Remember the sound of the wind seeping into the smallest places. Finding Its way in. Into you. The way It makes love into life, into you.

(*passionately, as a warning*) Nonviolence—if it's to be effective in that moment and long into the future—nonviolence must maintain love for the oppressor. <u>Love</u> <u>your</u> <u>enemies</u>. (*pleading*) As best as you can. <u>Love</u> <u>your</u> <u>enemies</u>. Awaken every torturer to love.

(*curtain drops fast*)

THE END

A BEGINNING

Bible Translation Fragment
Matthew 5:38-41
Jesus's nonviolent jujitsu

Jesus's "take nothing for the journey" (Mark 6, Matthew 10, Luke 9) invites people to live as Jesus himself lived and to trust as Jesus himself trusted.

Taking nothing for the journey, one must rely on the generosity of others and offer only whatever is within oneself in return—perhaps the gift of one's presence, one's wholeness, one's healing.

Living in this way, even for a short time, we come to discover a very different economy, a very different flow to life.

<u>Economy</u> derives from a Greek word/phrase... "taking care of one's house/family."

Who lives within your house? Whom do you include?

If you choose to be houseless—a bordercrossing wanderer—one's home is the whole world. One's economy—one's household for which to care—then includes everyone, every creature, the whole Earth.

But...what to do when someone does not share a vision of being neighbors/family with you or anyone else? What to do when someone wants to hold power over you?

As we know from *Jesus Plays*, Jesus has some ideas....

A New Translation of Matthew 5:38-41

You've heard it said: "An eye for an eye!" and "A tooth for a tooth!"

(Jesus likely here quotes the Torah...Exodus 21... though the Torah-writers quote Hammurabi's code, more ancient than anything in the Bible by a millennia..."an eye for an eye" was a Babylonian law enacted within their vast empire to minimize the violence brought on by vengeance, retribution, getting even with someone for an offense...which is to say you couldn't knock out two teeth if someone knocked out only one of your teeth)

And I say (egō de lēgō)...

...do not <u>set yourself up against</u> (antistēnai) <u>*anyone who annoys you with their wicked ways*</u> (ponērō).

Instead...

...whoever slaps you on your right cheek—to shame you publicly—turn the other one to that person—make them slap you with their other hand, which would bring shame upon the slapper in the ancient world...

...and for the one bringing you to trial to take your underclothes and all that is yours (chitōn: the garment worn so close to one's skin it symbolizes one's naked self), *permit that person to have your society-ranking outerclothes as well...*

...and whoever forces you into service one thousand paces, go and lead on for that person two thousand!

* * * * *

Ha ha ha ha ha...how Jesus helps us find ways out of such dicey situations with humor!

Hammurabi (in c 1755 BCE and perhaps others before him) simply sought to limit violence with "an eye for an eye." The Torah-assemblers of a few centuries before Jesus's time included this piece of Hammurabi's code as good sense for even their own religio-political society. But centuries after the Torah-writers, Jesus ups the ante. If someone bitchslaps you and if bitchslapping them back would likely get you killed because the one who slaps you has all the power, accept that first slap but use its energy to transform the entire situation. How? Jesus envisions accepting the first offense, rolling coolly with it, throwing off the oppressor's advance so you're both on level terrain with each other, and then moving in such a way as to ensure this offense never happens again. This is jujitsu.

While Jesus was crafting his wisdom saying for first century people living in his area of the world and in his time, a time and region under Roman occupation, Jesus invites ancient and modern hearers alike to transform situations where we are made the opponent and where we might make anyone our opponent. How? Engage Wisdom and level the playing field...with play...wise play that encourages oppressor and oppressed alike to realize together human equality under God, within God. Any altercation could then be an awakening for oppressor and oppressed alike, an awakening that invites both to welcome a new relationship with each other through an ever-larger knowledge of God/Universe in which both oppressor and oppressed live and move and have their being.

In the sayings and parables in *Jesus Plays*, Jesus seems most interested in deflating empires and our needs for them. "You are the light of the world"... Jesus reminds us. Note that Jesus wasn't exclusively recognizing this light within a king/caesar or president or high priest or CEO, hierarchs of Jesus's day or ours. Jesus did not say that we get our light through the light shining first through some king or president or religious leader or CEO. The light of the world is "you/plural"..."we" as in all of us. Note how so much of Christianity today wants us to see Jesus as the light of the world...even while he reminds us that we are all light...as much as farmers who plant dandelions for a living....as much as women who wrestle 45 pounds of dough and add yeast.

These parables or a wisdom saying like Matthew 5:38-41 seem so fresh and original and could get us closer to knowing something more "authentic" of Jesus, if that's important for you or me. More importantly, sayings/parabless like these could help us to realize that Wisdom is breathing life at the banquet table we all share...especially when we bring forward sayings/parables like these into the present moment in generative ways, as I hope *Jesus Plays* invites. After all, a wisdom saying or parable is not shared to be followed word for word but instead to invite creativity—to invite the hearer to create something new for oneself and maybe even for the the teller...to remind us all of Wisdom, life, the Universe, God...the larger/infinite world of possibilities, the deep mystery of life.

It seems a strange thing—and yet likely accurate—to say that the old gospels themselves often might take us further afield from Jesus. Sometimes the entire purpose of a gospel is to pick an argument with another gospel. Take, for instance, the Gospel of John and the Gospel of Thomas, two very different gospels which seem to be in active conversation with one another. Who doubts in the Gospel of John? Thomas, of course. John's signs-rich and speech-rich gospel argues for following Jesus and believing in Jesus as the keys to living a Godly life; Thomas's sayings-gospel argues for studying some sayings, discovering their patterns and somatic nuance/play, and then creating one's own sayings to invoke thinking/play into some current moment. Thomas's gospel is onto the very activity of generative Wisdom; John's gospel has little interest in Wisdom—John's gospel has no real wisdom sayings/parables and is instead more interested in having us follow Jesus/God.

Read for yourself both the Gospel of John and the Gospel of Thomas and you'll quickly discover the vast differences in imagination between these two gospel-communities and their very different understandings of Jesus. We readers would be wise to follow neither of these gospels—nor any gospel—without careful reflection. Following anything without reflection, as we know, is dangerous.

Of course, there is some rich middle ground here: Jesus seems interested in trusting God—as John's gospel advises—and in playing with Wisdom—as Thomas's gospel advises too. Maybe the wise learn to trust God/life more readily by studying Wisdom, the very nature of things...like the ways of the life-giving wind.

Wisdom, after all, is an inside-game that becomes relational. It's not about following someone's wisdom saying or the teller of the saying.

A good wisdom saying or parable unravels within the hearer to grow one's paradigm or understanding of life. A wisdom saying or parable does not tell us what to do but grows our discovery that we have choices and, as adults, we can create more choices. A wisdom saying or parable reminds us we no longer have to be toddlers who scream when our choices seem so limited, when we don't get what we want. As adults, we can reflect, create, discern, choose...all on one's own. Certainly, we can be informed by others' ideas...but an adult must choose for oneself.

And yet, rather wildly, Wisdom comes from going along slowly, dawdling, being an unrushed toddler again...

falling in love with a flower not because some poem or some work of art told you to notice it but because you or I find the flower on the way and become curious about its look, the ways it changes in the light or dances in the breeze, the flower's smell or taste, the ways the flower relates with the bees or bugs, the way the flower feels between one's fingers, the sound it might make if one dares crush it and smear it between one's hands and then onto the wall or sidewalk or my own arm or face or yours. We discover soon if this smearing is a good idea, not because a parent/adult corrects us but because it brought us or our play-companion or the flower itself joy or not. And so we learn.

May all who understand
laugh and delight from the rooftops!

Resources for the Journey

on the sayings of Jesus:
The Gospel of Jesus: According to the Jesus Seminar. Robert W. Funk, Arthur J. Dewey, & the Jesus Seminar. Salem, OR: Polebridge, 2015.

on the context of Jesus's parables:
Hear Then the Parable: A Commentary on the Parables of Jesus. Bernard Brandon Scott. Minneapolis: Augsburg, 1989.

on Jesus's nonviolent jujitsu:
Engaging the Powers: Discernment and Resistance in a World of Domination. Walter Wink. Minneapolis: Fortress, 1992.

on nonviolent success, one example of many in history:
Stride Toward Freedom: The Montgomery Story. Martin Luther King, Jr. New York: Harper & Bros, 1958.

on the oral nature of Jesus's world:
Orality and Literacy: The Technologizing of the Word. Walter J. Ong. New York: Routledge, 2012.

on similarities with Jesus's parables and Genesis:
A Wildly Sensual YAHWEH: The Controversial Genesis Stories in the Bible. Brian J. Shircliff. Cincinnati: VITALITY, revised 2024.

on YAHWEH as the wind, the ancient storm divinity first honored by the Shasu people:
The Invention of God. Thomas Römer. Cambridge, MA: Harvard, 2015.

About the Playwright & Translator

In addition to *The Naked Path of Prophet* series and now *Naked Little Fictions*, Brian Shircliff is the poet of *winds of (r)evolution* (paintings by Matthew Klooster) and author of the graphic novel *YAHWEH IS THE WIND!* (illustrated by Sean K. Long). Having taught high school religion for seventeen years, he felt the need to swim away from the shipwreck of organized religion for a more inclusive perspective, where the wind blows freely and surprisingly. He is a Bones for Life® Trainer, Guild Certified Feldenkrais Practitioner®, Healing Touch Certified Practitioner, and thirty-year student of many styles of meditation, tai chi, and yoga. He co-founded and continues to direct VITALITY Cincinnati's donation-based holistic self-care programs.

About Licensing This Play

Reach out to Brian by calling VITALITY's phone number listed on **vitalitycincinnati.org**.

Licensing fees help VITALITY grow affordable, holistic, self-awakening programs in-person in Cincinnati and via Zoom around the world.

About the Series

Fiction stripped down to the barest essentials, with a sly, breeze-satisfying, naked smile.

vol 1: **2029** (*flash fiction*)
vol 2: **No Average Joseph** (*play*)
vol 3: **Jesus Plays*** (*play*)

That love may grow in our world...

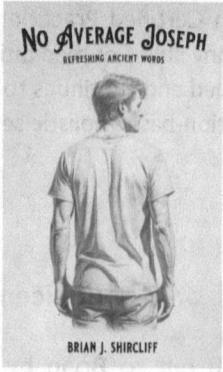

* While this play is a fiction—like any and every gospel is a fiction—the words of Jesus upon which this play is based are built upon the multi-decade work of the Jesus Seminar who has been trying to discern and distill what could be Jesus's authentic voice from what is more than likely the gospel writers' voices.

VITALITY...

**growing love,
sharing holistic self-care,
and inspiring creative expression.**

It's the power of a circle!

We invite you to explore with us through our

donation-based drop-in classes...
in person & via Zoom

affordable trainings

individual sessions

volunteer opportunities

vitalitycincinnati.org

VITALITY
buzz, bliss + books

publishing books from VITALITY's circle of friends
inspiring love, creativity, + possibility

vitalitybuzz.org

www.ingramcontent.com/pod-product-compliance
Lightning Source LLC
Chambersburg PA
CBHW011239120626
46549CB00009B/3340